WOMEN IN STEM
CHIEN-SHIUNG WU
FIRST LADY OF PHYSICS

by Clara MacCarald

Ideas for Parents and Teachers

Pogo Books let children practice reading informational text while introducing them to nonfiction features such as headings, labels, sidebars, maps, and diagrams, as well as a table of contents, glossary, and index.

Carefully leveled text with a strong photo match offers early fluent readers the support they need to succeed.

Before Reading
- "Walk" through the book and point out the various nonfiction features. Ask the student what purpose each feature serves.
- Look at the glossary together. Read and discuss the words.

Read the Book
- Have the child read the book independently.
- Invite him or her to list questions that arise from reading.

After Reading
- Discuss the child's questions. Talk about how he or she might find answers to those questions.
- Prompt the child to think more. Ask: Had you heard of Chien-Shiung Wu before reading this book? What more would you like to learn about her life or work?

Pogo Books are published by Jump!
5357 Penn Avenue South
Minneapolis, MN 55419
www.jumplibrary.com

Copyright © 2024 Jump!
International copyright reserved in all countries. No part of this book may be reproduced in any form without written permission from the publisher.

Library of Congress Cataloging-in-Publication Data is available at www.loc.gov or upon request from the publisher.

ISBN: 979-8-88996-698-2 (hardcover)
ISBN: 979-8-88996-699-9 (paperback)
ISBN: 979-8-88996-700-2 (ebook)

Editor: Katie Chanez
Designer: Emma Almgren-Bersie

Photo Credits: Science History Images/Alamy, cover (foreground), 1, 4, 6–7, 20–21; zizou7/Shutterstock, cover (atom); Shutterstock, cover (background); Dmitry Melnikov/Shutterstock, 3; pingebat/Shutterstock, 5; Everett Collection/Shutterstock, 8; Everett Collection Inc/Alamy, 9; Alexey Dozmorov/iStock, 10–11; Bjoern Wylezich/Shutterstock, 11; STOCKFOLIO®/Alamy, 12–13; Album/Alamy, 14–15; Bettmann/Getty, 16–17, 19; BioFoto/Shutterstock, 18; xpixel/Shutterstock, 23.

Printed in the United States of America at Corporate Graphics in North Mankato, Minnesota.

TABLE OF CONTENTS

CHAPTER 1
Small Town Girl..4

CHAPTER 2
The Atomic Age..8

CHAPTER 3
Famous in Physics..18

ACTIVITIES & TOOLS
Try This!..22
Glossary...23
Index...24
To Learn More...24

CHAPTER 1
SMALL TOWN GIRL

Chien-Shiung Wu was born in China in 1912. Her family lived in a small town. It was near Shanghai. At the time, many Chinese girls did not go to school. But Chien-Shiung did. Her parents thought girls should learn just like boys.

Chien-Shiung went to **college** in Nanjing. She studied **physics**. She was top of her class. She finished college in 1934.

CHAPTER 1 5

She worked in a physics lab after college. But she wasn't done learning. She decided to go to the United States. She went to **graduate school** at the University of California, Berkeley. After, she taught physics.

DID YOU KNOW?

Chien-Shiung **immigrated** to California in 1936. She took a ship.

CHAPTER 1

CHAPTER 1

CHAPTER 2
THE ATOMIC AGE

World War II started in 1939. The United States entered the war in 1941. Many countries were trying to make **atomic bombs**. These would be powerful weapons. They would release a lot of **radiation**. Whoever made them first might win the war.

atomic bomb

The U.S. government started the Manhattan Project. Its goal was to make atomic bombs. It was a secret project. Only the best scientists were asked to work on it.

Manhattan Project buildings

CHAPTER 2

uranium mine

Chien-Shiung joined the project in 1944. She worked on tools that measured radiation.

Some atomic bombs used **uranium**. This is what made them explode. There are different uranium **atoms**. Only one kind would work.

uranium ore

CHAPTER 2 · 11

Chien-Shiung helped find a way to separate the uranium atoms. Scientists used the right kind to make a bomb. The United States dropped two bombs on Japan in 1945. This helped end the war.

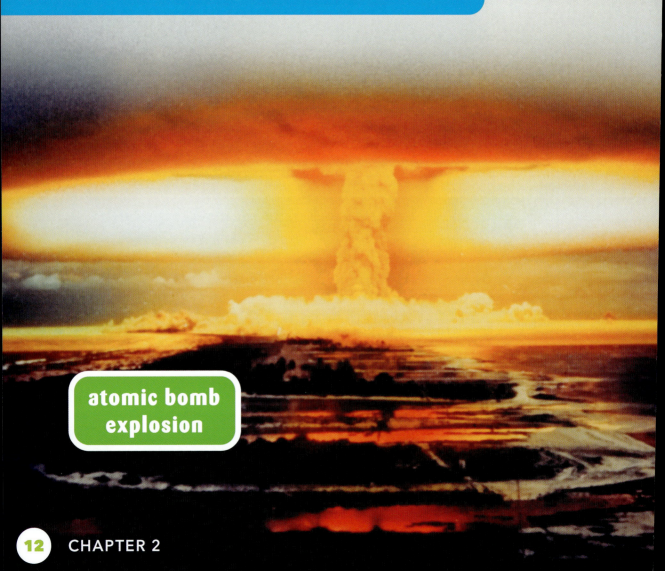

atomic bomb explosion

CHAPTER 2

TAKE A LOOK!

What are atoms made of? Take a look!

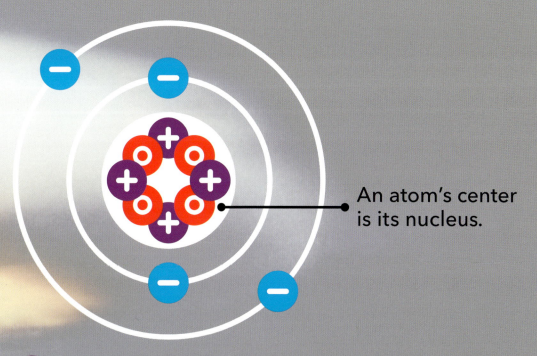

An atom's center is its nucleus.

➕ Protons are **particles**. They have a positive **charge**.

⭕ Neutrons are particles. They do not have a charge.

➖ Electrons are particles. They have a negative charge.

CHAPTER 2

In 1956, two scientists asked Chien-Shiung for help. They were Tsung-Dao Lee and Chen Ning Yang. They studied a type of radiation. They asked her to create an experiment. They wanted to test a physics **theory**.

CHAPTER 2

CHAPTER 2

CHAPTER 2

Chien-Shiung made the experiment. She carefully measured radiation. The experiment changed how people understand physics.

In 1957, the men received the **Nobel Prize** for the discovery. Chien-Shiung did not. Why? Many felt she was left out because she was a woman.

DID YOU KNOW?

Chien-Shiung Wu's experiment is named after her. It is called the Wu Experiment.

CHAPTER 2　17

CHAPTER 3
FAMOUS IN PHYSICS

Chien-Shiung kept working. She made more discoveries. She did important work in medicine. She studied blood cells.

blood cells

She was respected. She received many awards. People call her the "First Lady of Physics."

CHAPTER 3 19

Chien-Shiung **retired** in 1981. She spoke in public. She wanted girls to study science, too.

She died in 1997. Chien-Shiung is now famous. She is honored in China.

DID YOU KNOW?

In 1990, Chinese scientists named an **asteroid** after Chien-Shiung.

CHAPTER 3

ACTIVITIES & TOOLS

TRY THIS!

FINDING RADIATION

Chien-Shiung worked on tools that sense radiation. One is called a Geiger counter. Some click when they sense radiation. If there are low levels of radiation, it clicks slowly. If there are high levels, it clicks faster. Try this activity and pretend to use a Geiger counter!

What You Need:
- friend or family member
- small object to hide, like a toy
- stopwatch
- paper
- pen or pencil

❶ Have someone hide a small object. This person will be the Geiger counter.

❷ Imagine the object is giving off radiation.

❸ Have the Geiger counter make clicking noises.

❹ Use the stopwatch to measure 10 seconds. How many clicks did the Geiger counter make? Write the number down.

❺ Start looking for the object. Stop often. Have the Geiger counter click each time. The clicks should be slow when you are far from the object. They should speed up when you get closer.

❻ Write the number down each time. Compare the numbers as you look for the object.

❼ Once you find the object, try the game again. This time, be the Geiger counter. Why do you think sensing radiation is important?

GLOSSARY

asteroid: A small, rocky object that travels around the Sun.

atomic bombs: Weapons that create explosions by splitting atoms.

atoms: The smallest bits of pure matter.

charge: An electric state.

college: A place that teaches higher learning beyond high school.

graduate school: A school for people who have graduated college and are continuing their studies.

immigrated: Moved from one country to live in another.

Nobel Prize: A special award given to someone who does important things for the world.

particles: Extremely small parts of something.

physics: The study of energy and matter.

radiation: The act of giving off energy.

retired: Stopped working, usually after reaching a certain age.

theory: An idea or statement that explains how something happens.

uranium: A metal that gives off radiation and is used to make some atomic bombs.

World War II: A war in which the United States, Australia, France, Great Britain, the Soviet Union, and other nations defeated Germany, Italy, and Japan.

Geiger counter

ACTIVITIES & TOOLS

INDEX

asteroid 20
atomic bombs 8, 9, 11, 12
atoms 11, 12, 13
China 4, 5, 20
college 5, 6
experiment 14, 17
graduate school 6
immigrated 6
lab 6
Lee, Tsung-Dao 14, 17
Manhattan Project 9, 11
medicine 18
Nobel Prize 17
particles 13
physics 5, 6, 14, 17, 19
radiation 11, 14, 17
retired 20
scientists 9, 12, 14, 20
theory 14
University of California, Berkeley 6
uranium 11, 12
World War II 8, 12
Yang, Chen Ning 14, 17

TO LEARN MORE

Finding more information is as easy as 1, 2, 3.

1. Go to www.factsurfer.com
2. Enter "Chien-Shiung Wu" into the search box.
3. Choose your book to see a list of websites.

24 ACTIVITIES & TOOLS